Is This a Baby Dinosaur?

and other science picture-puzzles
by Millicent E. Selsam

Illustrated with photographs

Harper & Row, Publishers   New York   Evanston   San Francisco   London

To Patricia, Michael, Russell, Scott, and Andrew

SOURCES OF PHOTOGRAPHS

p. 3 James Welgos from National Audubon Society; *p. 4* lentil plant, Harold Krieger; *p. 5* Lynwood M. Chace from National Audubon Society; *p. 6* Hugh Spencer from National Audubon Society; *pp. 7-10* Treat Davidson from National Audubon Society; *p. 11* Gordon Smith from National Audubon Society; *p. 12* E. Javorsky from National Audubon Society; *p. 13* Gordon S. Smith from National Audubon Society; *p. 14* Beth Bergman from National Audubon Society; *p. 15* Lynwood M. Chace from National Audubon Society; *p. 16* owl head, Lynwood M. Chace from National Audubon Society; owl in flight, G. Ronald Austing from National Audubon Society; *p. 17* Ed Cesar from National Audubon Society; *p. 18* crested porcupine, Arthur Ambler from National Audubon Society; *p. 19* Jeanne White from National Audubon Society; *p. 20* scarlet runner bean germinating, Jeanne White; bean seedling, Hugh Spencer—both from National Audubon Society; scarlet runner bean plant, Jerome Wexler; *p. 21* Robert F. Seymour from National Audubon Society; *p. 22* Lynwood M. Chace from National Audubon Society; *p. 23* John H. Gerard from National Audubon Society; *p. 24* potato plants, Jerome Wexler; *pp. 25-26* Leonard Lee Rue from National Audubon Society; *pp. 27-28* Allan D. Cruickshank from National Audubon Society; *p. 29* R. F. Head from National Audubon Society; *p. 30* Jeanne White from National Audubon Society; *p. 31* Jack Dermid from National Audubon Society. *Front cover,* Allan D. Cruickshank from National Audubon Society.

Library of Congress Catalog Card Number: 72-76508
Trade Standard Book Number: 06-025302-9
Harpercrest Standard Book Number: 06-025303-7

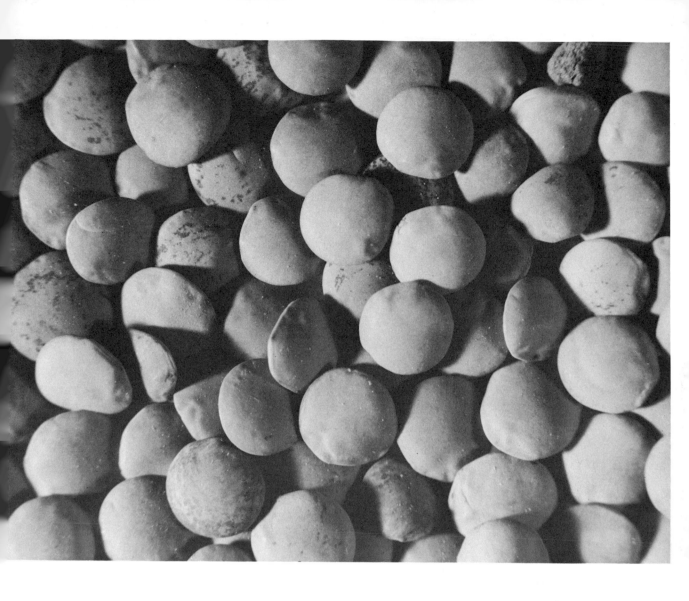

1711091

Are these pebbles?

No.
They are lentil seeds,
the kind that make good lentil soup.

Seeds can grow, but pebbles cannot.
When a lentil seed is planted,
roots grow down into the ground,
and green leaves and stems, like these,
grow up into the air.
But what happens if you plant a pebble? Nothing.

Could you put these on your Christmas tree?

No.
They wouldn't last.
They are the dewdrops on a spider web.
The spider catches insects
in the sticky threads of the web.

6

Could you string these into a necklace?

They would be too soft.
They are the eggs of trout—a fish that lives
in freshwater brooks and lakes.
Here you can see the young fish
growing inside the eggs. The two big black spots
in each egg are the eyes.

When the baby trout hatches out of the egg,
a sac of yolk from the egg stays attached to it.
The yolk sac has food for the baby fish.
The little fish uses this food for a few weeks,
while it is growing bigger.

When the trout are grown up, they look like this.

Whose neck is this?

It is not a giraffe's neck.
The neck of a giraffe is bigger and longer
and has big spots.

Here is the owner of the neck.

It is an ostrich, a big bird that cannot fly.
But it can run very fast on the open land
of the African plains.

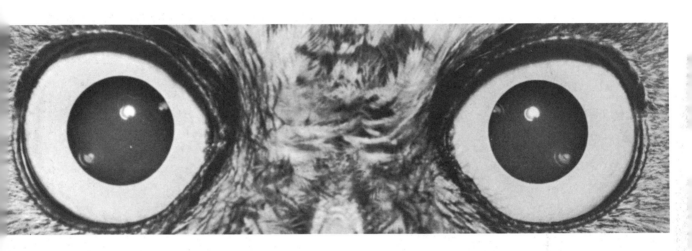

Are these two fried eggs?

No.
They are the eyes
of the great horned owl.

The owl can see very well at night
because its eyes are large
and catch every bit of the weak light.
Owls hear very well too.
They can hear mice rustling around in the leaves
of the forest floor. Owls eat mice.

Is this a rocket
streaking up into
the sky?

It is the tip of a porcupine's quill.
This is the way it looks under a magnifying glass.

The quills are very loosely attached
to the porcupine's skin. Porcupines do not throw
their quills. But the quills break off easily
and get into the skin of any animal
that attacks the porcupine.

18

Is this a lizard?

It is really a bean seed sprouting.
The roots you see here grow into the ground.

After the roots
grow into the ground,
the top part
of the bean plant grows.

In about two months
it will be
a bean plant like this.

Are these ferns growing in a forest?

No.
They are the designs
frost made on a windowpane.
The water vapor in the air of a room
hit the cold window
and formed crystals of ice.

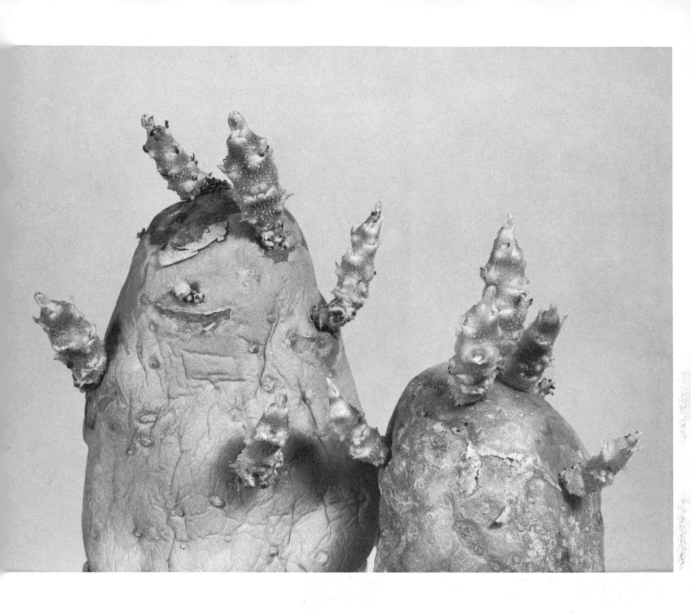

Are these two puppets?

You could use them for puppets,
but they are really potatoes
with buds growing out of them.

Every eye on the potato
has a bud that can grow
into stems and leaves
and become a potato plant.

The potatoes form
under the ground.

Is this an old broken tire?

25

No.
It is the horn of the desert bighorn sheep.
The sheep can attack another animal with its horns.
And it can protect itself with its horns,
when it is attacked.

Are these baby dinosaurs?

They are baby pelicans.

Here is a grown-up pelican sitting on the water.

Here is a pelican flying through the air.

The pelican has a big pouch
which holds the fish it catches.

Look hard at anything you see.
Is it what it seems to be?

Sometimes it is.

Sometimes it isn't.